Around Town

Shapes

T0004896

James D. Anderson

Consultants

Chandra C. Prough, M.S.Ed.
National Board Certified
Newport-Mesa
Unified School District

Jodene Smith, M.A.
ABC Unified School District

Publishing Credits

Dona Herweck Rice, *Editor-in-Chief*
Lee Aucoin, *Creative Director*
Chris McIntyre, M.A.Ed., *Editorial Director*
James Anderson, M.S.Ed., *Editor*
Aubrie Nielsen, M.S.Ed., *Associate Education Editor*
Neri Garcia, *Senior Designer*
Stephanie Reid, *Photo Editor*
Rachelle Cracchiolo, M.S.Ed., *Publisher*

Image Credits

p.5 Juri Bizgajmer/Dreamstime; p.8 Natalia Bratslavsky/Dreamstime; p.12 Photolibrary; p.28 Michael DeLeon/iStockphoto; All other images: Shutterstock

---

Teacher Created Materials
5301 Oceanus Drive
Huntington Beach, CA 92649-1030
http://www.tcmpub.com

ISBN 978-1-4333-3438-2
© 2012 Teacher Created Materials, Inc.
Printed in China
Nordica.072019.CA21901006

Table of Contents

Around Town 4

You Try It! 24

Solve the Problem 28

Glossary 30

Answer Key 32

Shapes are all around.

Find the shapes around town.

This is a **rectangle.**

A rectangle has four sides.

A rectangle has four **corners.**

Find the rectangles.

This is a **square.**

A square has four **equal** sides.

A square has four corners.

Find the squares.

This is a **triangle.**

A triangle has three sides.

A triangle has three corners.

Find the triangles.

This is a **circle.**

A circle is round.

A circle has no corners.

Find the circles.

Find shapes.

Find the shapes around town!

YOU TRY IT!

Can you find the circles?

Can you find the squares?

E

YOU TRY IT!

Can you find the rectangles?

Can you find the triangles?

YIELD

ADMIT
ONE
575 108
575 108

SOLVE THE PROBLEM

How can you use craft sticks to make shapes?

Materials

✓ craft sticks

✓ glue

1 Make a rectangle.

2 Make a square.

3 Make a triangle.

4 Can you make a circle?

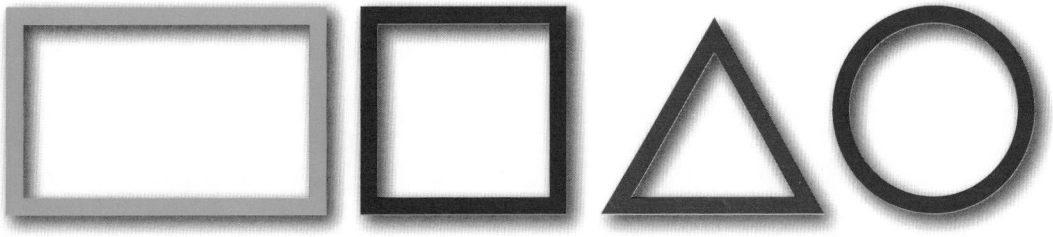

Glossary

circle—a round shape with no sides and no corners

corners—the points where two sides meet

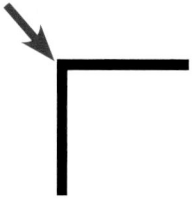

equal—the same length